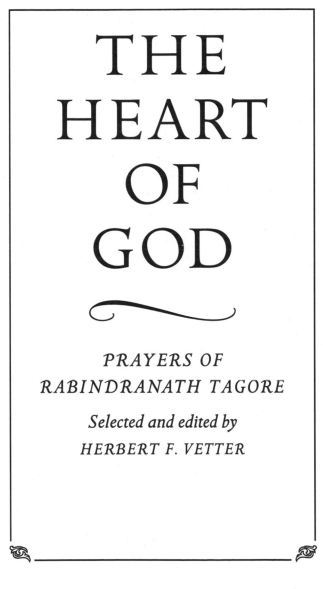

THE HEART OF GOD

PRAYERS OF RABINDRANATH TAGORE

Selected and edited by
HERBERT F. VETTER

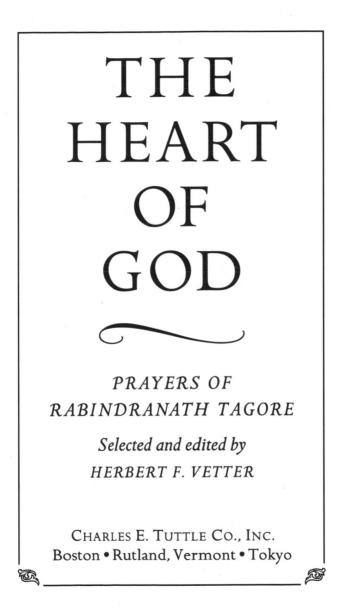

THE HEART OF GOD

PRAYERS OF
RABINDRANATH TAGORE

Selected and edited by
HERBERT F. VETTER

CHARLES E. TUTTLE CO., INC.
Boston • Rutland, Vermont • Tokyo

First published in 1997 by Tuttle Publishing, an imprint of Periplus Editions (HK) Ltd.,
with editorial offices at 153 Milk Street, Boston, Massachusetts 02109.

The text on pages ix-x was taken from *Indian Thought and Its Development*, by
Albert Schweitzer, copyright © 1936 by the Beacon Press.
The photograph on the back cover and the frontispiece is by LLAMAS, Boston.

ISBN: 0-8048-3125-4
The LCC number is on file with the Library of Congress.

DISTRIBUTED BY

USA
Charles E. Tuttle Co., Inc.
RR 1 Box 231-5
North Clarendon, VT
05759
tel.: (800) 526-2778
fax: (800) FAX-TUTL

JAPAN
Tuttle Shokai Ltd.
1-21-13, Seki
Tama-ku, Kawasaki-shi
Kanagawa-ken, 214
Japan
tel.: (044) 833-0225
fax: (044) 822-0413

SOUTHEAST ASIA
Berkeley Books Pte. Ltd.
5 Little Road #08-01
Singapore 536983
tel.: (65) 280-3320
fax: (65) 280-6290

First edition
05 04 03 02 01 00   99 98 97   1 3 5 7 9 10 8 6 4 2

∿

Cover design by Christopher Kuntze
Book design by Jill Winitzer

Printed in the United States of America

CONTENTS

~

FOREWORD

Modern Indian thought makes a noble attempt to get really clear about itself in Rabindranath Tagore. Born in 1861, he is at the same time thinker, poet, and musician. He has himself translated his important works into English. The attention of Europe was directed to him by his becoming the recipient of the Nobel Prize for Literature in 1913. For many years he lived at Santiniketan, in Bengal, where he built up a school and college on modern educational lines.

With Tagore, ethical world and life affirmation has completely triumphed. It governs his worldview and will suffer nothing of world and life negation beside it. This has all the significance of a really great deed. A process of development that has been going on for centuries reaches in him its natural conclusion. He demands that we should belong to God with the soul and serve God actively in the world.

Joy in life and joy in creation belong, according to Tagore, to our human nature. He is as little able as the others who had attempted it before him to really found the worldview of ethical affirmation on knowledge of the universe. But the Goethe of India gives expression to his personal experience that this is the truth in a manner more profound and more powerful and more charming than anyone had ever done before. This completely noble and harmonious thinker belongs not only to his own people but to humanity.

—*Albert Schweitzer*

INTRODUCTION

All the black evils in the world have overflowed their banks,

Yet, oarsmen, take your places with the blessing of sorrow in your souls!

Whom do you blame, brothers? Bow your heads down!

The sin has been yours and ours.

The heat growing in the heart of God for ages—

The cowardice of the weak, the arrogance of the strong, the greed of fat prosperity, the rancour of the wronged, pride of race, and insult to man—

Has burst God's peace, raging in storm.

I first found these lines during World War II— and have never forgotten them. After the war, when I sought more of Tagore's work, I first encountered his prayers of power. With what other literature of my acquaintance might they be compared? I saw kinship with the enduring majesty and inner depths of the Hebrew Psalms, yet happily they avoided the latter's recurring vindictiveness. I felt Tagore's passionate, profoundly personal I-Thou experience akin to that expressed in the Confessions of Augustine, yet he was no ally of St. Augustine's intense negation of both life and the world. The prayers of the modern Poet of India did and do celebrate life in spite of its abundance of tragedy, and they affirm our world of ever enduring, ever changing harmonies of color and sound.

When I met Amiya Chakravarty, an Indian and American scholar who once was Tagore's literary secretary, he encouraged my quest to know more about this rare living legacy of prayer. I was clearly not alone in my appreciation of Tagore's contribution. Indeed, it was precisely such work as the prayers in this small book that led to Rabindranath's becoming the first Asian to be awarded the Nobel Prize for Literature in 1913. The Nobel Committee considered and passed over Tolstoy, Ibsen, Strindberg, Yeats, and George Bernard Shaw. The award symbolized the uncommon strength of Tagore's simple prayers of common life. Indeed, in his introduction to Rabindranath Tagore's first English writings, *Gitanjali* (Song Offerings), W. B. Yeats tells us that when he was carrying the manuscript with him as he traveled on trains and buses, he often had to close it lest some stranger see how much it moved him.

Tagore's poem prayers are moving affirmations of power that are not divorced from the tragedies of life. His mother died when he was thirteen. He lost his wife when she was only thirty. Soon thereafter, he experienced the death of a daughter as well as that of his father and his youngest son. Even before this devastating series of events came the disturbing death of his beloved sister-in-law, Kadambari, who took her own life. Rabindranath himself years later experienced a period of such depression and despair that he, too, considered ending his own life.

Nevertheless, like the fabled Phoenix bird arising from the ashes, Rabindranath emerged as a world-renowned person of power. Consider the astounding range of the work of this poet who was born in the mansion of a culturally distinguished Calcutta family on May 7, 1861. He was an educator who as a child so intensely hated going to school that he refused to continue to go, but he later established a liberating school for children at his family estate 100 miles from Calcutta in a place named by his father, the Abode of Peace. He later also founded there, in Santiniketan, an international university, Visva-Bharati, designed to foster an ongoing meeting of East and West to facilitate a creative synthesis of the arts and sciences, re-creating civilization. As if that were not enough, in Tagore's lifelong labor to free his ailing country from domination by the British Empire, he helped establish lively centers of education for India's overwhelmingly illiterate population then living in poverty and disease-struck rural villages all across the land. The poet believed that India, the birthplace of such historic world religions as Hinduism and Buddhism, must meet the challenge of creative response to the Western civilization that was choking its development. He carried forward his father's and grandfather's leadership of the Hindu reform movement, known as the Brahmo Samaj, a major facilitator of the Indian Renaissance. He not only affirmed his Indian roots in the ancient Vedas, he affirmed that the Buddha was the greatest human being who ever lived; he extolled the Christian virtues of the Sermon on the Mount; and he translated the poems of Kabir, the daringly innovative mystic seer of Islam.

This exemplar of a new renaissance of Indian and world civilization lived an astonishingly adequate life. He was a poet and educator, a playwright and actor, a composer and singer, as well as a painter, essayist, novelist, and author of short stories. He was also both a social reformer who created a center for rural reconstruction and a world traveler who spoke to citizens of many nations in both the East and the West: China, Japan, Russia, the United States, France, Britain, Holland, Switzerland, Germany, Austria, Italy, Czechoslovakia, Norway, Sweden, Denmark, Bulgaria, Persia, Egypt, and Greece. And he was an honored visitor to Southeast Asia, delighted to note the continuing impact of ancient India among these neighbors.

Shortly before Tagore's death in 1941 in Calcutta at the age of eighty, the chief justice of India presented this rebel ally of Mahatma Gandhi with an honorary doctorate awarded by Oxford University. The citation noted that the myriad-minded Dr. Tagore did not hold himself aloof from the dust and heat of the world; he did not fear to challenge the British Raj itself and the authority of the British Empire's magistrates. Tagore appreciatively accepted this recognition of his life work as "a happy augury of an Age to come."

I think humanity increasingly will honor the treasury of prayers breathed by this international exemplar of sacred power that is somewhere-nowhere-everywhere always. With this purpose in mind, I have prepared this deliberately small volume of durable literature presented in a form suitable for present-day use. Titles have been added to each selection. Whenever it was occasionally necessary to degenderize the text, I have done so in the spirit of Tagore. I have also edited the prayers in the language of contemporary daily speech, thereby avoiding such archaic obstacles as thee and thou.

The sources from which I have drawn these selections are *Gitanjali* (1912), *The Gardener* (1913), *Sadhana* (1913), *Fruit-Gathering* (1916), *Stray Birds* (1916), *Crossing* (1918), and *The Fugitive and Other Poems* (1921).

My own labor has been lightened by the excellent publication of *The English Writings of Rabindranath Tagore*, edited by Sisir Kumar Das: Volume 1, *Poems* (1994); Volume 2, *Plays, Stories, Essays* (1996).

For those who may be interested, there is a major admiring but sharply demythologizing biography published in 1995 entitled *Rabindranath Tagore: The Myriad-Minded Man*, by Krishna Dutta and Andrew Robinson.

I wish to thank my esteemed colleagues in ministry who advised me on the Tagore prayers as part of a larger project: Dr. Arthur Foote of S.W. Harbor, Maine; Professor John F. Hayward of Southern Illinois University; the Reverend Kenneth Read-Brown of the First Parish (Old Ship Church) in Hingham, Massachusetts; and the Reverend Bruce Southworth of the Community Church of New York. Esteemed advisors in the field of publishing include Jeanette Hopkins, Gobin and Julia Stair, Marie Cantlon, and the staff of Michael Kerber, at Tuttle Publishing.

Finally, the spirit of *The Heart of God: Prayers of Rabindranath Tagore* may be symbolized by a single sentence by Sarvepalli Radhakrishnan, the distinguished philosopher and statesman who served as president of India:

Rabindranath Tagore was one of the few representatives of the universal person to whom the future of the world belongs.

—H.F.V.
Cambridge, Massachusetts
April 23, 1997

PRAYERS

ACCEPT ME

Accept me, dear God, accept me for this while.

Let those orphaned days that passed without You be forgotten.

Only spread this little moment wide across Your lap, holding it under Your light.

I have wandered in pursuit of voices that drew me, yet led me nowhere.

Now let me sit in peace and listen to Your words in the soul of my silence.

Do not turn away Your face from my heart's dark secrets, but burn them till they are alight with Your fire.

~

A QUESTION TO GOD

Age after age, O God, You have sent Your messengers into this pitiless world, who have left their word: "Forgive all. Love all. Cleanse your hearts from the blood-red stains of hatred."

Adorable are they, ever to be remembered; yet from the outer door, I have turned them away today—this evil day—with unmeaning salutation.

Have I not seen secret malignance strike down the helpless under the cover of hypocritical might?

Have I not heard the silenced voice of justice weeping in solitude at might's defiant outrages?

Have I not seen in what agony reckless youth, running mad, has vainly shattered its life against insensitive rocks?

Choked is my voice, mute are my songs today, and darkly my world lies imprisoned in a dismal dream; and I ask You, O God, in tears, "Have You Yourself forgiven, have even You loved those who are poisoning Your air and blotting out Your light?"

~

ARE YOU ABROAD?

Are You abroad on this stormy night on Your journey of love, my Friend? The sky groans like one in despair.

I have no sleep tonight. Ever and again I open my door and look out on the darkness, my Friend.

I can see nothing before me. I wonder where Your path lies.

By what dim shore of the ink-black river, by what far edge of the frowning forest, through what mazy depth of gloom are You treading Your course to come to me, my Friend?

~

WHY?

At midnight the would-be ascetic announced: "This is the time to give up my home and seek God. Ah, who has held me so long in delusion here?"

God whispered, "I," but the ears of the man were stopped.

With a baby asleep at her breast lay his wife, peacefully sleeping on one side of the bed.

The man said, "Who are you that have fooled me so long?"

The voice again said, "They are God," but he heard it not.

The baby cried out in its dream, nestling close to its mother.

God commanded, "Stop, don't leave your home," but still he heard not.

God sighed and complained, "Why does my servant wander to seek me, forsaking me?"

~

TREES

Be still, my heart, these great trees are prayers.

~

MY GREETINGS

Comrade of the road, here are my traveler's greetings to You.

God of my broken heart, of leave-taking and loss, of the gray silence of the dayfall, my greetings of the ruined house to You.

Light of the newborn morning, sun of the everlasting day, my greetings of undying hope to You.

My Guide, I am a wayfarer on an endless road, my greetings of a wanderer to You.

~

FACE TO FACE?

Day after day, O Ruler of my life, shall I stand before You face to face?

With folded hands, O Ruler of all worlds, shall I stand before You face to face?

Under Your great sky, in solitude and silence with humble heart, shall I stand before You face to face?

In this laborious world of Yours, tumultuous with toil and with struggle, among hurrying crowds, shall I stand before You face to face?

And when my work shall be done in this world, O Ruler of rulers, alone and speechless, shall I stand before You face to face?

~

DEATH

Death, Your servant, is at my door. He has crossed the unknown sea and brought Your call to my home.

The night is dark, and my heart is fearful—yet I shall take up the lamp, open my gates, and bow to him my welcome. It is Your messenger who stands at my door.

I shall worship him with folded hands and with tears. I shall worship him, placing at his feet the treasure of my heart.

~

HOLD MY HAND

Deliver me from my own shadows, O God, from the wreck and confusion of my days, for the night is dark and Your pilgrim is blinded.

Hold my hand.

Deliver me from despair.

Touch with Your flame the lightless lamp of my sorrow.

Waken my tired strength from its sleep.

Do not let me linger behind, counting my losses.

Let the road sing to me of the house at every step.

For the night is dark, and Your pilgrim is blinded.

Hold my hand.

≈

DELIVERANCE

Deliverance is not for me in renunciation.
I feel the embrace of freedom in a thousand bonds
of delight.

You ever pour for me the fresh draft of Your
wine of various colors and fragrances, filling this
earthen vessel to the brim.

My world will light its hundred different lamps
with Your flame and place them before the altar of
Your temple.

No, I will never shut the doors of my senses.
The delights of sight and hearing and touch will
bear Your delight.

Yes, all my illusions will burn into
illumination of joy, and all my desires ripen into
fruits of love.

～

THIS IS MY PRAYER

Give me the supreme courage of love, this is my prayer—the courage to speak, to do, to suffer at Your will, to leave all things or be left alone. Strengthen me on errands of danger, honor me with pain, and help me climb to that difficult mood that sacrifices daily to You.

Give me the supreme confidence of love, this is my prayer—the confidence that belongs to life in death, to victory in defeat, to the power hidden in the frailest beauty, to that dignity in pain which accepts hurt but disdains to return it.

~

THE POOREST

Here is Your footstool, and there rest Your feet
where live the poorest, the lowliest, and lost.

When I try to bow to You, my obeisance
cannot reach down to the depth where Your feet
rest among the poorest, the lowliest, and lost.

Pride can never approach where You walk in
the clothes of the humble among the poorest, the
lowliest, and lost.

My heart can never find its way to where You
keep company with the companionless among the
poorest, the lowliest, and lost.

～

TIME TO SIT QUIETLY

I ask for a moment's indulgence to sit by Your side. The works that I have in hand I will finish afterward.

Away from the sight of Your face, my heart knows no rest or respite, and my work becomes an endless toil in a shoreless sea of toil.

Today the summer has come at my window with its sighs and murmurs; and the bees are plying their minstrelsy at the court of the flowering grove.

Now it is time to sit quietly, face to face with You, and to sing dedication of life in this silent and overflowing leisure.

~

THE REBEL

I came nearest to You, though I did not know it, when I came to hurt You.

I owned You at last as my Master when I fought against You to be defeated.

I merely made my debt to You burdensome when I robbed You in secret.

I struggled in my pride against Your current, only to feel all Your force in my breast.

Rebelliously, I put out the light in my house, and Your sky surprised me with its stars.

~

THE LEAST GRAIN OF CORN

I had gone a-begging from door to door in the village path, when Your golden chariot appeared in the distance like a gorgeous dream, and I wondered who was this King of all kings!

My hopes rose high, and I thought my evil days were at an end. I stood waiting for alms to be given unasked and for wealth to be scattered on all sides in the dust.

The chariot stopped where I stood. Your glance fell on me, and You came down with a smile. I felt that the luck of my life had come at last. Then all of a sudden You held out Your right hand, saying, "What have you to give me?"

Ah, what a kingly jest was it to open Your palm to a beggar to beg! I was confused and stood undecided, and then from my wallet I slowly took out the least little grain of corn and gave it to You.

How great was my surprise when at the day's end, I emptied my bag on the floor only to find a least little grain of gold among the poor heap! I bitterly wept and wished that I had the heart to give You my all.

~

MY FRIEND

I have come to You to take Your touch before I begin my day.

Let Your eyes rest upon my eyes for a while.

Let me take to my work the assurance of Your comradeship, my Friend.

Fill my mind with Your music to last through the desert of noise.

Let Your love's sunshine kiss the peaks of my thoughts and linger in my life's valley where the harvest ripens.

~

MY POLAR STAR

I have made You the polar star of my existence; never again can I lose my way in the voyage of life.

Wherever I go, You are always there to shower Your beneficence all around me. Your face is ever present before my mind's eyes.

If I lose sight of You even for a moment, I almost lose my mind.

Whenever my heart is about to go astray, just a glance of You makes it feel ashamed of itself.

≈

WISDOM

I have scaled the peak and found no shelter in fame's bleak and barren height.

Lead me, my Guide, before the light fades, into the valley of quiet where life's harvest mellows into golden wisdom.

~

YOUR PRESENCE

I know not from what distant time You are ever coming nearer to meet me.

Your sun and Your stars can never keep You hidden from me forever.

In many a morning and evening, Your footsteps have been heard, and Your messenger has come within my heart and called me in secret.

I know not why today my life is all astir, and a feeling of tremulous joy is passing through my heart.

It is as if my time were come to wind up my work, and I feel in the air a faint sweet smell of Your presence.

~

TREASURES

I know that the day will come when my sight of this earth shall be lost, and life will take its leave in silence, drawing the last curtain over my eyes.

Yet stars will watch at night, and morning rise as before, and hours heave like sea waves casting up pleasures and pains.

When I think of this end of my moments, the barrier of the moments breaks, and I see by the light of death Your world with its careless treasures. Rare is its lowliest seat; rare is its meanest of lives.

Things that I longed for in vain and things that I got—let them pass. Let me but truly possess the things that I ever spurned and overlooked.

NOT ALTOGETHER LOST

I know that this life, missing its ripeness in love, is not altogether lost.

I know that the flowers that fade in the dawn, the streams that strayed in the desert, are not altogether lost.

I know that whatever lags behind, in this life laden with slowness, is not altogether lost.

I know that my dreams that are still unfulfilled, and my melodies still unstruck, are clinging to Your lute strings, and they are not altogether lost.

~

MY VOYAGE

I thought that my voyage had come to its end at the last limit of my power, that the path before me was closed, that provisions were exhausted and the time had come to take shelter in a silent obscurity.

But I find that Your will knows no end in me, and when old words die out on the tongue, new melodies break forth from the heart; and where the old tracks are lost, new country is revealed with its wonders.

YOUR NAME

I will utter Your name, sitting alone among
the shadows of my silent thoughts. I will utter it
without words; I will utter it without purpose. For
I am like a child that calls its mother a hundred
times, glad that it can say, "Mother."

~

YOU ARE THERE

I would leave this chanting and singing and telling of beads. Whom do I worship in this lonely dark corner of a temple with doors all shut? I open my eyes and see that, You, O God, are not before me.

You are there where the tiller is tilling the hard ground and where the pathmaker is breaking stones. You are with them in sun and in shower, and Your garment is covered with dust. I put off my holy mantle and even, like You, come down on the dusty soil.

Deliverance? Where is deliverance to be found? You Yourself have joyfully taken upon Yourself the bonds of creation; You are bound with us all forever.

I come out of my meditations and leave aside my flowers and incense. What harm if my clothes become tattered and stained? I meet You and stand by You in toil and in the sweat of my brow.

~

BEYOND DESPAIR

In desperate hope, I go and search for her in all the corners of my room; I find her not.

My house is small, and what once has gone from it can never be regained.

But infinite is Your mansion, my God; and seeking her, I have come to Your door.

I stand under the golden canopy of Your evening sky, and I lift my eager eyes to Your face.

I have come to the brink of eternity from which nothing can vanish—no hope, no happiness, no vision of a face seen through tears.

Oh, dip my emptied life into that ocean, plunge it into the deepest fullness. Let me, for once, feel that lost, sweet touch in the allness of the universe.

~

MY SONG

In my songs, I have voiced Your spring
flowers and given rhythm to Your rustling leaves.

I have sung into the hush of Your night and
the peace of Your morning.

The thrill of the first summer rains has passed
into my tunes and the waving of the autumn
harvest.

Let not my song cease.

~

SALUTATION

In one salutation to You, my God, let all my senses spread out and touch this world at Your feet.

Like a raincloud hung low with its burden of unshed showers, let all my mind bend down at Your door in one salutation to You.

Let all my songs gather together their diverse strains into a single current and flow to a sea of silence in one salutation to You.

Like a flock of homesick cranes flying night and day back to their mountain nests, let all my life take its voyage to its eternal home in one salutation to You.

~

THE SOLITARY WAYFARER

In the deep shadows of the rain, with secret steps, You walk, silent as night, eluding all watchers.

Today the morning has closed its eyes, heedless of the insistent calls of the loud east wind, and a thick veil has been drawn over the ever wakeful blue sky.

The woodlands have hushed their songs, and doors are shut at every house. You are the solitary wayfarer in this deserted street. Oh, my only Friend, my best Beloved, the gates are open in my house. Do not pass by like a dream.

~

SLEEP

In the night of weariness, let me give myself up to sleep without struggle, resting my trust upon You.

Let me not force my flagging spirit into a poor preparation for Your worship.

It is You who draws the veil of night upon the tired eyes of the day to renew its sight in a fresher gladness of awakening.

~

MOTHER EARTH

Infinite wealth is not Yours, my patient and dusky mother dust!

You toil to fill the mouths of Your children, but food is scarce.

The gift of gladness that You have for us is never perfect.

You cannot satisfy all our hunger hopes, but should I desert You for that?

Your smile, which is shadowed with pain, is sweet to my eyes.

Your love, which knows not fulfillment, is dear to my heart.

From Your breast You have fed us with life but not immortality, which is why Your eyes are ever wakeful.

For ages You are working with color and song, yet Your heaven is not built, but only its sad suggestion.

Over Your creations of beauty, there is the mist of tears.

I will pour my songs into Your tender face and love Your mournful dust, Mother Earth.

∼

ABOUNDING JOY

Is it beyond You to be glad with the gladness of this rhythm? To be tossed and lost and broken in the whirl of this fearful joy?

All things rush on, they stop not, they look not behind; no power can hold them back, they rush on.

Keeping steps with that restless, rapid music, seasons come dancing and pass away—colors, tunes, and perfumes pour in endless cascades in the abounding joy that scatters and gives up and dies every moment.

∼

WORKER OF THE UNIVERSE

It is only the revelation of You as the Infinite that is endlessly new and eternally beautiful in us and that gives the only meaning to our self when we feel Your rhythmic throb as soul-life, the whole world in our own souls; then are we free.

O Worker of the universe! Let the irresistible current of Your universal energy come like the impetuous south wind of spring; let it come rushing over the vast field of human life. Let our newly awakened powers cry out for unlimited fulfillment in leaf and flower and fruit.

～

MY LAST SONG

Let all the strains of joy mingle in my last song—the joy that makes the earth flow over in the riotous excess of the grass; the joy that sets the twin brothers, life and death, dancing over the wide world; the joy that sweeps in with the tempest, shaking and waking all life with laughter; the joy that sits still with its tears on the open, red lotus of pain; and the joy that throws everything it has upon the dust and knows not a word.

~

THE GRASP OF YOUR HAND

Let me not pray to be sheltered from dangers, but to be fearless in facing them.

Let me not beg for the stilling of my pain, but for the heart to conquer it.

Let me not crave in anxious fear to be saved, but hope for the patience to win my freedom.

Grant me that I may not be a coward, feeling Your mercy in my success alone; but let me find the grasp of Your hand in my failure.

~

LET MY SONG BE SIMPLE

Let my song be simple as the waking in the morning, as the dripping of dew from the leaves,

Simple as the colors in clouds and showers of rain in the midnight.

But my lute strings are newly strung, and they darken their notes like spears sharp in their newness.

Thus they miss the spirit of the wind and hurt the light of the sky, and these strains of my songs fight hard to push back Your own music.

~

MY ALL

Let only that little be left of me whereby I may name You my all.

Let only that little be left of my will whereby I may feel You on every side and come to You in everything and offer to You my love every moment.

Let only that little be left of me whereby I may never hide You.

Let only that little of my fetters be left whereby I am bound with Your will, and Your purpose is carried out in my life—and that is the fetter of Your love.

~

MY COUNTRY

Let the earth and the water, the air and the fruits of my country be sweet, my God.

Let the homes and marts, the forests and fields of my country be full, my God.

Let the promises and hopes, the deeds and words of my country be true, my God.

Let the lives and hearts of the sons and daughters of my country be one, my God.

～

MY LAST WORD

Let this be my last word, that I trust in Your love.

~

YOUR LOVE

Let Your love play upon my voice and rest on my silence.

Let it pass through my heart into all my movements.

Let Your love, like stars, shine in the darkness of my sleep and dawn in my awakening.

Let it burn in the flame of my desires and flow in all currents of my own love.

Let me carry Your love in my life as a harp does its music, and give it back to You at last with my life.

~

LIFE OF MY LIFE

Life of my life, I shall ever try to keep my body pure, knowing that Your living touch is upon all my limbs.

I shall ever try to keep all untruths from my thoughts, knowing that You are that truth which has kindled the light of reason in my mind.

I shall ever try to drive all evils away from my heart and keep my love in flower, knowing that You have Your seat in the inmost shrine of my heart.

It shall be my endeavor to reveal You in my actions, knowing it is Your power that gives me strength to act.

~

LIGHT

Light, my light, the world-filling light, the eye-kissing light, the heart-sweetening light:

Ah, the light dances, my Darling, at the center of my life; the light strikes, my Darling, the chords of my love; the sky opens; the wind runs wild; laughter passes over the earth.

The butterflies spread their sails on the sea of light. Lilies and jasmine surge up on the crest of the waves of light.

The light is shattered into gold on every cloud, my Darling, and it scatters gems in profusion.

Mirth spreads from leaf to leaf, my Darling, and gladness without measure. The heaven's river has drowned its banks, and the flood of joy is abroad.

~

THE FULLNESS OF PEACE

Not for me is the love that knows no restraint and is like foaming wine that, having burst its vessel in a moment, would run to waste.

Send me the love that is cool and pure like Your rain, which blesses the thirsty earth and fills the homely earthen jars.

Send me the love that would soak down into the center of being, and from there would spread like the unseen sap through the branching tree of life, giving birth to fruits and flowers.

Send me the love that keeps the heart still with the fullness of peace.

~

OBSTINATE ARE THE SHACKLES

Obstinate are the shackles, and my heart aches when I try to break them.

Freedom is all I want; but to hope for it, I feel ashamed.

I am certain that priceless wealth is in You and that You are my best friend, but I have not the heart to sweep away the tinsel that fills my room.

The shroud that covers me is a shroud of dust and death; I hate it, yet hug it in love.

My debts are large, my failures great, my shame secret and heavy; yet when I come to ask for my good, I quake in fear lest my prayer be granted.

~

LOST TIME

On many an idle day I have grieved over lost time, but it is never lost, O God. You have taken every moment of my life in Your own hands.

Hidden in the heart of things, You are nourishing seeds into sprouts, buds into blossoms, and ripening flowers into fruitfulness.

I was tired and sleeping on my idle bed and imagined all work had ceased. In the morning, I awoke and found my garden full with wonders of flowers.

~

THE INFINITY
OF YOUR LOVE

Stand before my eyes, and let Your glance touch my songs into a flame.

Stand among Your stars, and let me find kindled in their lights my own fire of worship.

The earth is waiting at the world's wayside.

Stand upon the green mantle she has flung upon Your path, and let me find in her grass and meadow flowers the spread of my own salutation.

Stand in my lonely evening when my heart watches alone; fill her cup of solitude, and let me feel in myself the infinity of Your love.

～

I WANT YOU, ONLY YOU

That I want You, only You—let my heart repeat without end. All desires that distract me, day and night, are false and empty to the core.

As the night keeps hidden in its gloom the petition for light, even thus in the depth of my unconsciousness rings the cry "I want You, only You."

As the storm still seeks its end in peace when it strikes against peace with all its might, even thus my rebellion strikes against Your love and still its cry is "I want You, only You."

~

RAIN

The day is dim with rain.

Angry lightning glances through the tattered cloud-veils, and the forest is like a caged lion shaking its mane in despair.

On such a day amid the winds beating their wings, let me find my peace in Your presence.

For the sorrowing sky has shadowed my solitude, to deepen the meaning of Your touch about my heart.

~

DARKNESS AND LIGHT

The lantern that I carry in my hand makes an enemy of the darkness of the farther road.

And this wayside becomes a terror to me, where even the flowering tree frowns like a spectre of scowling menace; and the sound of my own steps comes back to me in the echo of muffled suspicion.

Therefore, I pray for Your own morning light, when the far and the near will kiss each other, and life will be one in love.

~

THE STREAM OF LIFE

The same stream of life that runs through my veins night and day runs through the world and dances in rhythmic measures.

It is the same life that shoots in joy through the dust of the earth in numberless blades of grass and breaks into tumultuous waves of leaves and flowers.

It is the same life that is rocked in the ocean-cradle of birth and of death, in ebb and in flow.

I feel my limbs made glorious by the touch of this world of life. And my pride is from the life-throb of ages dancing in my blood this moment.

~

STRIKE AT THE ROOT

This is my prayer to You, O God—strike, strike at the root of poverty in my heart.

Give me the strength to bear lightly my joys and sorrows.

Give me the strength to make my love fruitful in service.

Give me the strength never to disown the poor or bend my knees before insolent might.

Give me the strength to raise my mind high above daily trifles.

Give me the strength to surrender my strength to Your will with love.

~

THANKSGIVING

Those who walk on the path of pride,
crushing the lowly life under their tread, covering
the tender green of the earth with their footprints
in blood,

Let them rejoice and thank You, God, for the
day is theirs.

But I am thankful that my lot lies with the
humble who suffer and bear the burden of power
and hide their faces and stifle their sobs in the
dark.

For every throb of their pain has pulsed in the
secret depth of Your night, and every insult has
been gathered into Your great silence;

And the morrow is theirs.

. . .

O Sun, arise upon the bleeding hearts
blossoming in flowers of the morning, and the
torchlight revelry of pride shrunken to ashes.

~

TAKE, O TAKE

Time after time I came to Your gate with raised hands, asking for more and yet more.

You gave and gave, now in slow measure, now in sudden excess.

I took some, and some things I let drop; some lay heavy on my hands; some I made into playthings and broke them when I tired, till the wrecks and the hoard of Your gifts grew immense, hiding You, and the ceaseless expectation wore my heart out.

"Take, O take" has now become my cry.

Hold my hands; raise me from the still-gathering heap of Your gifts into the bare infinity of Your uncrowded presence.

~

TIME

Time is endless in Your hands, O God. There is none to count Your minutes.

Days and nights pass, and ages bloom and fade like flowers. You know how to wait.

Your centuries follow one another in perfecting a small wildflower.

We have no time to lose, and having no time, we must scramble for our chances. We are too poor to be late.

Thus it is that time goes by, while I give it to every querulous person who claims it, and Your altar is empty of all offerings to the last.

At the end of the day, I hasten in fear lest the gate be shut, but I find that there is yet time.

~

TEARS OF THE EARTH

We rejoice, O God, that the tears of the earth keep her smiles in bloom.

~

WHAT DIVINE DRINK

What divine drink would You have, my God, from this overflowing cup of my life?

My Poet, is it Your delight to see Your creation through my eyes, to stand at the portals of my ears, to listen silently to Your own eternal harmony?

Your world is weaving words in my mind, and Your joy is adding music to them. You give Yourself to me in love and then feel Your own entire sweetness in me.

~

THE MUSIC OF LOVE

When all the strings of my life will be tuned,
then at every touch of Yours will come out the
music of love.

~

NO NIGHT OF EASE

When I awake in Your love, my night of ease will be ended.

Your sunrise will touch my heart with its touchstone of fire, and my voyage will begin in its orbit of triumphant suffering.

I shall dare to take up death's challenge and carry Your voice into the heart of mockery and menace.

I shall bare my breast against the wrongs hurled at Your children and take the risk of standing by Your side, where none but You remains.

～

O WORLD

When my heart did not kiss You in love,
O World, Your light missed its full splendor and
Your sky watched through the long night with its
lighted lamp.

My heart came with her songs to Your side,
whispers were exchanged, and she put her wreath
on Your neck.

I know she has given You something which
will be treasured with Your stars.

~

PLAYTIME

When my play was with You, I never questioned who You were. I knew no shyness or fear; my life was boisterous.

In the early morning, You would call me from my sleep like my own comrade and lead me running from glade to glade.

On those days, I never cared to know the meaning of songs You sang to me. Only my voice took up the tunes, and my heart danced in their cadences.

Now, when the playtime is over, what is this sudden sight that is come upon me? The world, with eyes bent upon Your feet, stands in awe with all its silent stars.

~

WHEN THE HEART IS HARD

When the heart is hard and parched, come upon me with a shower of mercy.

When grace is lost from life, come with a burst of song.

When tumultuous work raises its din on all sides, shutting me out from beyond, come to me, God of silence, with Your peace and rest.

When my beggarly heart sits crouched, shut up in a corner, break open the door, my God.

When desire blinds the mind with delusion and dust, O Holy One, come with Your light and Your thunder.

~

SINGING

When You command me to sing, it seems that my heart would break with pride; and I look to Your face, and tears come to my eyes.

All that is harsh and dissonant in my life melts into one sweet harmony—and my adoration spreads wings like a glad bird on its flight across the sea.

I know You take pleasure in my singing. I know that only as a singer I come before Your presence.

I touch, by the edge of the far-spreading wing of my song, Your feet, which I could never aspire to reach.

Drunk with the joy of singing, I forget myself, and call You Friend who is my Ruler.

~

WHEN YOU SAVE ME

When You save me, the steps are lighter in the march of Your worlds.

When stains are washed away from my heart, it brightens the light of Your sun.

That the bud has not blossomed in beauty in my life spreads sadness in the heart of creation.

When the shroud of darkness will be lifted from my soul, it will bring music to Your smile.

～

LET MY COUNTRY AWAKE

Where the mind is without fear, and the head is held high;

Where knowledge is free;

Where the world has not been broken up into fragments by narrow domestic walls;

Where words come out from the depth of truth;

Where tireless striving stretches its arms toward perfection;

Where the clear stream of reason has not lost its way into the dreary desert sand of dead habit;

Where the mind is led forward by You into ever widening thought and action—

Into that haven of freedom, my Father, let my country awake.

~

NOTHING BUT YOUR LOVE

Yes, I know, this is nothing but Your love, O Beloved of my heart—this golden light that dances upon the leaves, these idle clouds sailing across the sky, this passing breeze leaving its coolness upon my forehead.

The morning light has flooded my eyes—this is Your message to my heart. Your face is bent from above, Your eyes look down on my eyes, and my heart has touched Your feet.

~

THE SKY AND THE NEST

You are the sky, and You are the nest as well.

Beautiful One, there in the nest Your love encloses the soul with colors and sounds and odors.

There comes the morning, with the golden basket in her right hand bearing the wreath of beauty, silently to crown the earth.

And there comes the evening over the lonely meadows deserted by herds, through trackless paths, carrying cool drafts of peace in her golden pitcher from the western ocean of rest.

But there, where spreads the infinite sky for the soul to take her flight in, reigns the stainless white radiance. There is no day or night, no form or color, and never, never a word.

~

NOW IN THE EVENING

You have given me a seat at Your window from the early hour.

I have spoken to Your silent servants of the road running on Your errands and have sung with Your choir of the sky.

I have seen the sea in calm, bearing its immeasurable silence, and in storm, struggling to break open its own mystery of depth.

I have watched the earth in its prodigal feast of youth and in its slow hours of brooding shadows.

Those who went to sow seeds have heard my greetings, and those who brought their harvest home, or their empty baskets, have passed by my songs.

Thus at last my day has ended, and now in the evening, I sing my last song to say that I have loved Your world.

~

GIFTS

You have given me Your love, filling the world with Your gifts.

They are showered upon me when I do not know them, for my heart is asleep, and dark is the night.

Though lost in the cavern of my dreams, I have been thrilled with gladness;

And I know that in return for the treasure of Your great worlds, You will receive from me one little flower of love in the morning when my heart awakes.

~

YOU HAVE MADE ME ENDLESS

You have made me endless, such is Your pleasure. This frail vessel You empty again and again, and fill it ever with fresh life.

This little flute of a reed You have carried over hills and dales and have breathed through it melodies eternally new.

At the immortal touch of Your hands, my little heart loses its limits in joy and gives birth to utterance ineffable.

Your infinite gifts come to me only on these very small hands of mine. Ages pass, and still You pour, and still there is room to fill.

~

FRIENDS WHOM I KNEW NOT

You have made me known to friends whom I knew not. You have given me seats in homes not my own. You have brought the distant near and made a brother of the stranger.

I am uneasy at heart when I have to leave my accustomed shelter; I forget that there abides the old in the new and that there also You abide.

Through birth and death, in this world or in others, wherever You lead me, it is You, the same, the one Companion of my endless life, who links my heart with bonds of joy to the unfamiliar.

When one knows You, then alien there is none, then no door is shut. O grant me my prayer that I may never lose the bliss of the touch of the one in the play of the many.

YOU HIDE YOURSELF

You hide Yourself in Your own glory, O God.
The sand-grain and the dewdrop are more
proudly apparent than You are.

The world unabashed calls all things his own
that are Yours—yet it is never brought to shame.

You make room for us while standing aside in
silence; wherefore, love lights her own lamp to
seek You and comes to Your worship unbidden.

⁓

FREED AT LAST!

You took my hand and drew me to Your side, made me sit on the high seat before all others, till I became timid, unable to stir and walk my own way, doubting and debating at every step lest I should tread upon any thorn of their disfavor.

I am freed at last!

The blow has come, the drum of insult sounded, my seat is laid low in the dust.

My paths are open before me.

My wings are full of the desire of the sky.

I go to join the shooting stars of midnight, to plunge into the profound shadow.

I am like the storm-driven cloud of summer that, having cast off its crown of gold, hangs as a sword the thunderbolt upon a chain of lightning.

In desperate joy I run upon the dusty paths of the despised; I draw near to Your final welcome.

The child finds its mother when it leaves her womb. When I am parted from You, thrown out from Your household, I am free to see Your face.

~

ETERNAL TRAVELER

You will find, Eternal Traveler, marks of Your
footsteps across my songs.

~

WORSHIP

Your gifts to us mortals fulfill all our needs and yet run back to You undiminished.

The river has its everyday work to do and hastens through the fields and hamlets; yet its incessant stream winds toward the washing of Your feet.

The flower sweetens the air with its perfume; yet its last service is to offer itself to You.

Your worship does not diminish the world.

From the words of the poet, people take what meanings please them; yet their last meaning points to You.

～

THE PERFECT UNION

Your joy in me is full.

You have taken me as Your partner of all this wealth. In my heart is the endless play of Your delight. In my life, Your will is ever taking shape.

You who are the Ruler of rulers have decked Yourself in beauty, and Your love loses itself in the love of Your lover in the perfect union of two.

~

YOUR LIGHT, MY LIGHT

Your light, my light, world-filling light, the dancing center of my life, the sky breaks forth, the wind runs wild, and laughter passes over the earth.

The butterflies have spread their sails to glide up on the seas of light; the lilies and the jasmine flowers surge on the crest of waves of light.

Now heaven's river drowns its banks, and floods of joy have run abroad; now mirth has spread from leaf to leaf, and gladness without measure comes.

~

YOUR SUNBEAMS

Your sunbeams come upon this earth of mine with arms outstretched and stand at my door the livelong day to carry back to Your feet clouds made of my tears and sighs and songs.

With fond delight, You wrap about Your starry breast that mantle of misty cloud, turning it into numberless shapes and folds and coloring it with hues ever changing.

It is so light and so fleeting, tender and tearful and dark, that is why You love it, O Serene One, and that is why it may cover Your awful white light with its shadows of Your suffering.

~

YOURS

Yours is the light that breaks forth from the dark, and the good that sprouts from the deft heart of strife.

Yours is the house that opens upon the world, and the love that calls to the battlefield.

Yours is the gift that still is a gain when everything is a loss, and the life that flows through the caverns of death.

Yours is the heaven that lies in the common dust, and You are there for me; You are there for all.

~